MAKO SHRKS

The Amazing World of Sharks

BLUE SHARKS

BULL SHARKS

DEEPWATER SHARKS

FRESHWATER SHARKS

GREAT WHITE SHARKS

HAMMERHEAD SHARKS

MAKO SHARKS

RAYS

THRESHER SHARKS

TIGER SHARKS

The Amazing World of Sharks

MAKO SHARKS

By Elizabeth Roseborough

MC MASON CREST

Mason Crest
450 Parkway Drive, Suite D
Broomall, Pennsylvania 19008
(866) MCP-BOOK (toll-free)
www.masoncrest.com

First printing
9 8 7 6 5 4 3 2 1
Printed in the USA

ISBN (hardback) 978-1-4222-4128-8
ISBN (series) 978-1-4222-4121-9
ISBN (ebook) 978-1-4222-7677-8

Library of Congress Cataloging-in-Publication Data

Names: Roseborough, Elizabeth, author.
Title: Mako sharks / Elizabeth Roseborough.
Description: Broomall, Pennsylvania: Mason Crest, [2019] | Series: The amazing world of sharks | Includes bibliographical references and index.
Identifiers: LCCN 2018013891 (print) | LCCN 2018018313 (ebook) | ISBN 9781422276778 (eBook) | ISBN 9781422241288 (hardback) | ISBN 9781422241219 (series)
Subjects: LCSH: Mako sharks--Juvenile literature. | Mako sharks--Behavior--Juvenile literature.
Classification: LCC QL638.95.L3 (ebook) | LCC QL638.95.L3 R68 2019 (print) | DDC 597.3/3--dc23
LC record available at https://lccn.loc.gov/2018013891

Developed and Produced by National Highlights Inc.
Editors: Keri De Deo and Mika Jin
Interior and cover design: Priceless Digital Media
Production: Michelle Luke

QR CODES AND LINKS TO THIRD-PARTY CONTENT

CONTENTS

KEY ICONS TO LOOK FOR:

Words to Understand: These words with their easy-to-understand definitions will increase the reader's understanding of the text while building vocabulary skills.

Sidebars: This boxed material within the main text allows readers to build knowledge, gain insights, explore possibilities, and broaden their perspectives by weaving together additional information to provide realistic and holistic perspectives.

Educational Videos: Readers can view videos by scanning our QR codes, providing them with additional educational content to supplement the text. Examples include news coverage, moments in history, speeches, iconic sports moments, and much more!

Text-Dependent Questions: These questions send the reader back to the text for more careful attention to the evidence presented there.

Research Projects: Readers are pointed toward areas of further inquiry connected to each chapter. Suggestions are provided for projects that encourage deeper research and analysis.

Series Glossary of Key Terms: This back-of-the book glossary contains terminology used throughout this series. Words found here increase the reader's ability to read and comprehend higher-level books and articles in this field.

FUN FACTS...
GETTING TO KNOW THEM

TIGER SHARK
Named for the vertical striped markings along its body, but they fade with age.

MAKO SHARK
Known as the race car of sharks for its fast swimming speed!

BULL SHARK
Named for its stocky shape, broad, flat snout, and aggressive, unpredictable behavior!

RAYS
Rays and sharks belong to the same family. A ray is basically a flattened shark.

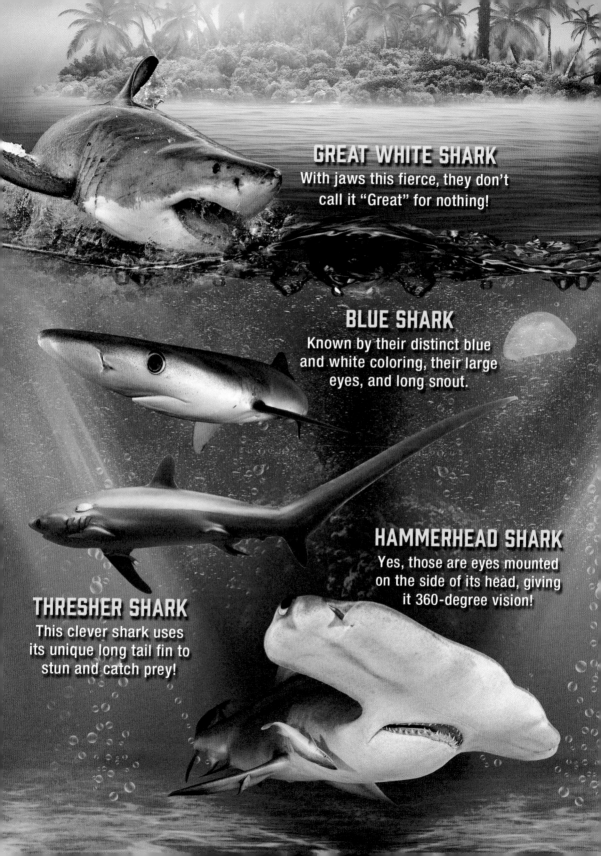

GREAT WHITE SHARK
With jaws this fierce, they don't call it "Great" for nothing!

BLUE SHARK
Known by their distinct blue and white coloring, their large eyes, and long snout.

HAMMERHEAD SHARK
Yes, those are eyes mounted on the side of its head, giving it 360-degree vision!

THRESHER SHARK
This clever shark uses its unique long tail fin to stun and catch prey!

WORDS TO UNDERSTAND:

apex predator: An animal at the top of its food chain, with no natural predators. The mako shark is an example of an apex predator.

breach: An action in which ocean animals propel their bodies out of the water. This behavior is typically exhibited during hunting.

captivity: A man-made habitat for animals (such as a zoo or aquarium). Animals are not able to leave captivity unless humans free them.

subtropical: A climate that is between tropical and temperate. Florida and some areas of the Mediterranean Sea are examples of subtropical climates.

CHAPTER 1

INTRODUCING MAKO SHARKS

The Michael Phelps of the ocean, the mako shark is the fastest shark on record, with speeds of up to 60 mph (about 97 kmph). For comparison's sake, the fastest humans in the world run about 20 mph (32 kmph). There are many factors that make the mako shark so fast. From their long, cylindrical snouts to their torpedo-shaped bodies, mako sharks are simply built for speed. Their large, muscular tails also help them propel through the water at lightning speed. Also known as the blue pointer shark and the bonito shark, mako sharks are found in tropical, subtropical, and temperate waters around the world. Mako sharks prefer swimming in the open ocean, and it's rare that they swim near shorelines.

Makos are built for speed.

SIDEBAR

WHERE DOES THE NAME *MAKO SHARK* COME FROM?

The word *mako* means shark. The word comes from the Maori people—an indigenous group of people from the Polynesian Islands. The mako shark holds special significance to the Maori because they believe that mako sharks are spirit animals who protect them. Tribal leaders even wear mako teeth as jewelry because they are highly valued in their culture.

The mako shark is most well-known for its speed, but it is also known for its fearlessness. Often, mako sharks sustain injuries when hunting their favorite food, swordfish. Many mako sharks have been found with swordfish bills (the pointy part of a swordfish's nose) impaled in their faces or gills. Mako sharks are also known for going after fishermen who hunt them. Sometimes, the sharks free themselves from the net or fishing hook and then jump on board the fishing boat, either attacking the fishermen or attempting to destroy the boat. While mako sharks are beautiful, they are also fierce.

A mako's favorite food is swordfish.

There are two different varieties of mako sharks: shortfin and longfin. These sharks are very similar. Scientists know a lot more about shortfin mako sharks, as they're more common and tend to swim closer to the surface of the ocean. It wasn't until the mid-1960s that scientists even realized that longfin mako sharks are a different species, and they are still learning more about these larger, deeper-swimming cousins of the shortfin mako shark.

Mako sharks are easily identifiable by their brilliant blue coloring, pointy noses, mouths full of teeth, and large, muscular tails. The dorsal (top) side of their bodies range from metallic blue to deep indigo, allowing them to easily blend in with the ocean's surface, making them nearly invisible to their prey (and to humans who could potentially harm them). This deep blue color is one of the hallmarks of mako sharks, and one of the things (other than their smaller size) that differentiate them from their close relatives, great white sharks.

Fishermen target the mako shark for its blue coloring.

This beautiful coloring makes the mako shark one of the most sought-after ocean animals for their skin. The bright blue coloring eventually fades into the brilliant white on the mako's belly. Many fishermen kill mako sharks to turn their skin into leather, and this is just one of the many reasons that the mako shark is nearly on the endangered species list. While mako shark fishing is legal in most areas, many scientists believe that this hunting needs to end to save the mako shark from becoming extinct. Much like the lion is the king of the jungle, the mako shark is one of the kings of the ocean. With no natural predators, the only animal mako sharks have to be afraid of is humans.

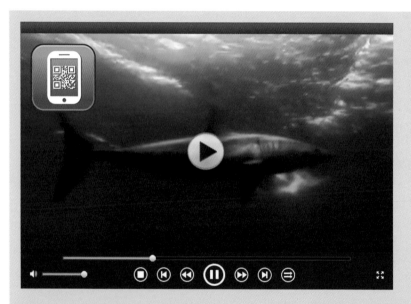

How are mako sharks able to swim so fast? Watch this video to learn about how their unique body shape and skin properties allow them to swim fast enough to catch their quick, agile prey.

Mako sharks are well known for the incredible show they put on when seen in the open ocean. It's very rare to see a mako shark near the shoreline. In order to see these sharks, it's essential to go out into the open ocean many miles from land obstacles. Mako sharks hunt vertically, meaning they start their attack from deep in the ocean, they accelerate, and surprise their prey before they know what hit them. Often, the mako shark preys on more than one animal at a time, often attacking entire schools of fish at once.

DO MAKO SHARKS ATTACK PEOPLE?

Mako sharks have been blamed for many attacks on people, but it's unlikely that they will attack unless they feel threatened or have been provoked. Often, makos swim behind fishing boats to eat the fish attracted to the fishermen's bait. Sometimes, this causes mako sharks to inadvertently get caught, often leading to attacks on humans after the shark is reeled onto the boat. Sometimes, mako sharks manage to free themselves from nets and hooks, and then will jump on the boat to attack the fishermen on board. While mako sharks are not typically looking for humans to attack, they will lash out if they feel that they are in danger.

In open water, mako sharks give many signs that they are about to attack. Typically, they swim in figure-eight patterns and approach their prey with their mouths open. It is extremely rare that a mako shark would ever attack a human unless they felt that their well-being was threatened. Remember, mako sharks rarely approach coastlines, as they prefer to swim in the open ocean. It's unlikely that anyone swimming or surfing near the shore would ever encounter a mako shark. Mako shark attacks are almost always the result of the shark getting caught in a fishing net or fishing line.

Mako sharks are also known to get defensive and aggressive if they feel that their prey is being threatened. They have been known to show violent behavior when fishing boats come near their half-eaten meals. Since makos are able to leap onto boats, it's important for fishermen to steer clear of makos that may be hunting.

Mako sharks prefer swimming in the deep ocean.

This octopus would make a good meal for a mako shark.

Mako sharks typically eat fatty animals without backbones such as squid and octopi, or bony fish such as tuna and mackerel. They are especially fond of swordfish. It's important that mako sharks attack swordfish quickly to avoid getting injured by the pointy spike that makes up a swordfish's nose. Many mako sharks are covered in scars from their fights with swordfish. While these fights between swordfish and mako sharks happen often, that does not stop the mako shark from going after its favorite food. They have also been known to attack animals such as sea birds, sea turtles, dolphins, porpoises, and seals, but this is not as common.

Often, the incredible burst of speed required to hunt causes the shark to breach the water and soar into the air—up to 20 ft. (6 m) —with the prey still in its mouth! Mako sharks do not make these great displays on purpose; it's likely that they are moving so fast while hunting that it's impossible for them to stop once they hit the surface of the water. Since it's likely for a mako to want to eat more than one animal when attacking a school of fish, it's actually not in the shark's best interest to breach the water, as this clearly alerts all other fish in the area of its presence.

Mako sharks are also known to breach the water when they are caught in a fisherman's net or fishing line. While it may be interesting to watch, it's actually quite sad because while putting on this display, mako sharks are trying to free themselves from the hooks in their mouths or untangle themselves from the nets, not put on a fancy show for people to watch. Many fishermen tell stories about mako sharks jumping on boats and attacking those on board. Some mako sharks have even been known to destroy the boats of the fishermen who were attempting to catch them by taking bites out of the boat. Humans often kill mako sharks, but they do not go down without a fight. When mako sharks do get away from fishermen, the sharks are often left with devastating injuries, such as hooks still being stuck in their mouths or nets being tangled around their fins, causing cuts when they move. When these injuries eventually result in death, it is not reported to fishing authorities, making it seem like the number of mako sharks killed by fishermen is much lower than in reality.

The mako is a large species of predatory shark that can grow up to 14.6 ft. (4.45 m).

SIDEBAR

SHARK MYTH: SHARKS HAVE NO PREDATORS

Humans are the most dangerous predators of sharks. While some sharks do have natural predators in the ocean, mako sharks do not because they are **apex predators**. Sport fishing is the number one killer of mako sharks. While it's difficult to imagine anyone standing up to a shark, many fishermen hunt sharks regularly. In order to stop sharks from going extinct, it's essential that shark fishing be regulated. It's important to note that although swordfish sometimes injure mako sharks, they are not considered predators. A swordfish will not attempt to eat a mako shark. When swordfish hurt makos, they are always doing so in self-defense, as they are attempting to escape the mako's grasp.

With one of the largest brain-to-body ratios of all fish, mako sharks are incredibly intelligent, and this intelligence helps them to be excellent hunters. Mako sharks are not the largest sharks in the ocean, but their intelligence helps them to be some of the most effective hunters. While most sharks rely on sensing electrical signals in the water to help them hunt, the mako shark simply relies on its excellent vision, hearing, and sense of smell to find its prey. Mako sharks have especially large eyes that help them to see well, even in areas of dark, murky water where other animals struggle to see potential predators or prey. When a mako shark attacks, it's nearly impossible for its prey to escape, as the shark's teeth are curved inward like hooks. Like most sharks, makos have many rows of teeth, and they are not hurt if they lose some teeth while attacking their prey. Typically, mako sharks do not use their teeth to do much chewing—their teeth are simply there for the attack. Most mako sharks either bite their prey in half before swallowing, or simply swallow their prey whole after they have completed their attack.

Mako sharks prefer to swim in the deep ocean, far from coastlines and people. This is one of the many reasons that mako sharks do not survive well in captivity. They need large, open spaces, and they do not understand how to keep themselves safe from running into walls and glass. In the open ocean, mako sharks love to swim—they are known for traveling up to 62 mi. (100 km) per day!

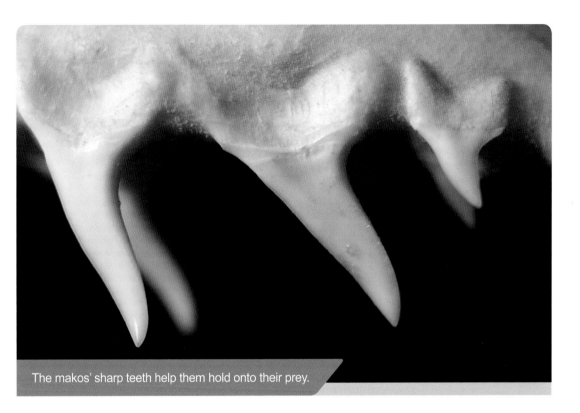

The makos' sharp teeth help them hold onto their prey.

TEXT-DEPENDENT QUESTIONS:

1. Do mako sharks jump out of the water on purpose?

2. What is the biggest threat to mako sharks?

3. How fast can mako sharks swim?

RESEARCH PROJECT:

In some countries, there are rules against hunting mako sharks. Research the laws about shark hunting in your area.

WORDS TO UNDERSTAND:

bycatch: Animals that are unintentionally caught with fishing nets or hooks during commercial fishing.

climate: The weather conditions that exist in an area over a long period of time.

habitat: The natural environment in which an animal lives.

pelagic: The pelagic zone is the open ocean that is not touching any land. Mako sharks prefer to stay between the surface and a maximum depth of 720 ft. (220 m).

CHAPTER 2

THE MAKO SHARK'S POPULATION AND HABITAT

HABITAT

Unlike many other sharks, mako sharks are not found all over the world. Mako sharks are typically known to make their habitats in temperate, subtropical, and tropical climates. They prefer water that is neither too hot nor too cold. In tropical regions, mako sharks tend to swim a bit deeper than they do in other regions, as the water near the surface of the ocean can be a bit too warm for their liking. They do an excellent job of finding

Like mako sharks, tuna are pelagic animals.

a suitable water temperature even as they travel through different climate regions. When mako sharks swim near the surface and breach in tropical waters, it's because they are either hunting or trying to free themselves from a fisherman's hook. A mako shark will put itself in the temporary discomfort of warmer waters when it is attacking prey. They are capable of hunting and surviving in colder waters, but it's unusual for mako sharks to venture away from the warm ocean. It's very rare for a mako shark to spend much time in water below 61°F (16.1°C).

Since mako sharks prefer to swim in the deep, open ocean, it's uncommon for them to come near a shoreline. Mako sharks that are found near the shoreline are often sick or starving, and they come toward the coast looking for food (usually to hunt for seals). Mako sharks are pelagic animals. Their main sources of prey—swordfish, tuna, and mackerel—are pelagic animals as well. This means that they like to swim in open water, without obstacles. This also explains why mako sharks tend to fare poorly in aquariums and zoos; they simply are not built to navigate obstacles such as glass and walls.

Watch this video to learn about the variety of animal life that lives in the pelagic zone of the ocean, between the ocean's surface and approximately 1,800 ft. (550 m) deep.

While mako sharks do not venture into the cold, polar waters of the Arctic and Antarctic circles, they are fairly widespread in warmer regions of the world. In the western Atlantic, mako sharks can be found off the coast of Chile in South America up to the waters of Nova Scotia in North America. In the eastern Atlantic, mako sharks can be found from Norway in Europe to South Africa, and throughout the Indian Ocean from South Africa to Australia.

Like many sharks, makos tend to stay as close to their favorite food—swordfish—as possible. Wherever a school of swordfish is swimming, it's likely that mako sharks are nearby. Often, scientists track schools of swordfish in order to help them locate and learn more about mako sharks. Swimming with swordfish can be dangerous for mako sharks, as large fishing companies often hunt swordfish, and mako sharks can be killed or injured in the fishing process.

POPULATION

Currently, the number of mako sharks left in the world is decreasing at a fairly rapid rate. It's hard for scientists to know the exact number of mako sharks that are left in the wild for a few reasons. Since mako sharks migrate frequently, when they leave one area it's hard to tell if they have died out, or have simply migrated to another area. Scientists are working hard to tag as many mako sharks as possible to learn more about them, but since mako sharks can be difficult (and dangerous) to tag, this is a slow process. Marine biologists have noticed a decline in mako shark sightings in areas that are usually filled with mako sharks, and areas that mako sharks used to frequent are not as highly populated. It's also important to note that mako shark fishing has increased significantly in the past few years, which is another reason scientists think the population is declining.

SIDEBAR

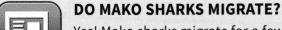

DO MAKO SHARKS MIGRATE?

Yes! Mako sharks migrate for a few different reasons. They migrate seasonally, moving to warmer areas during the fall and winter months. Makos will also migrate to follow food sources and when it's time to mate. While mako sharks are capable of swimming long distances, it's unusual for them to swim from one continent to another. Oddly enough, even though it is not typical for mako sharks to swim long distances, they do hold the record for fastest long-distance travel—one mako shark was recorded swimming 1,300 mi. (about 2,092 km) in just thirty-seven days! They typically stay in one region of the world, and move north and south as the weather changes. Marine biologists aren't sure how makos migrate exactly, but they do know that it's likely that female mako sharks migrate to warm waters when it's time to have pups. Newborn and very young mako sharks are often found off the coast of San Diego, California in the warm spring, summer, and early-autumn months. Pregnant sharks have plenty of time to make this journey, as they are typically pregnant from fifteen to eighteen months with eight to ten pups. Female mako sharks typically have babies every three years, and their migration patterns reflect this.

Since mako sharks are apex predators, it's clear that their numbers are not declining because of any natural causes. Other animals are not hunting them, and they are not dying out because they do not have enough to eat. There are a number of reasons for their population decline, and all of the issues are directly caused by humans, including finning, bycatch, and sport fishing.

CONSERVATION STATUS

The International Union for Conservation of Nature (IUCN) is an organization that works to protect plants and animals that are in danger of being eliminated from the earth. They study animals and plants with declining populations, and make recommendations on how to revitalize these populations. The IUCN has a system that determines how likely different species are to become extinct.

The IUCN has nine different categories of conservation status for plants and animals. The lowest two categories are not evaluated (NE) and data deficient (DD). These categories contain plants and animals that are so abundant that scientists are not currently studying their population numbers. The next category is least concern (LC). A plant or animal in this category is being watched, but is not currently at any risk of becoming extinct. The next category is near threatened (NT). Animals and plants in the NT category are likely to become extinct in the future if corrective action is not taken. Next is vulnerable (VU), and organisms in this category are close to becoming extinct, and corrective action must be taken to ensure that these populations do not disappear. The following category is endangered (EN). Animals and plants in this category are going to become extinct if current human behavior toward their species continues. Endangered animals and plants are dangerously close to disappearing from the earth. The next step is critically endangered (CR), which means that the species is incredibly close to becoming extinct in the very near future, and unless extreme corrective action is taken, disappearance

Extinct (EX)
Extinct in the Wild (EW)
Critically Endangered (CR)
Endangered (EN)
Vulnerable (VU)
Near Threatened (NT)
Least Concern (LC)
Data Deficient (DD)
Not Evaluated (NE)

is inevitable. The final two categories are extinct in the wild (EW) and extinct (EX). Species that are extinct in the wild exist in captivity, but not in the natural world. While this may seem promising, often, the animals in captivity have become used to human care and are unable to ever survive in the wild. Animals in captivity also tend to be less healthy and have shorter life spans than animals in the wild, regardless of how scientists attempt to replicate their natural diet and habitat. Plants and animals that are extinct no longer exist.

The mako shark is currently listed as vulnerable, which is the step below endangered. This means that if current fishing and conservation practices continue, the mako shark will eventually become extinct. This status is based on the population that marine biologists know of currently, but the exact number of mako sharks remaining is a bit tough to determine, as they frequently migrate and are difficult to catch and tag. Scientists are sure that there is not a natural cause creating a decline in the mako shark population. The numbers are decreasing solely due to human activity. It's important that humans take action to increase the number of mako sharks in the ocean. Many countries have laws that they believe will prevent overfishing of mako sharks, but currently, no countries have outlawed mako shark fishing entirely. There is nowhere in the world that provides a safe haven for makos, especially since they are unable to survive in captivity.

The mako shark's dorsal (top) fin is often used in shark fin soup, which is quite popular in Asia and parts of North America. In order for restaurants to get fins for soup, makos are sometimes the victims of a practice called finning. Finning is when a fisherman catches a mako shark, pulls the shark on board the fishing boat, cuts off the shark's dorsal fin with a sharp knife, and then dumps the shark back into the water. While this may seem more humane than killing the shark, the opposite is true. Without their dorsal fins, mako sharks are unable to swim quickly enough to catch their

Can you see the tag on this mako shark's dorsal fin? This will help researchers learn more about mako sharks.

HOW DO SCIENTISTS TAG MAKO SHARKS?

Tagging is a practice in which scientists attach a tracking device to a shark in order to help them learn more about the shark's behavior, habitat, and life span. While the tagging process is momentarily painful for the shark, it's important that scientists learn as much about makos as possible so that they can stop their population from becoming extinct. It can be quite dangerous for scientists to tag mako sharks, as the shark may feel threatened and attack the person attempting to place the tag. There are many different types of tags that scientists can attach to sharks. One of the most common is the acoustic tag. The acoustic tag is attached to the shark's dorsal fin. The tag regularly sends out pings, which are pulses of sound waves. These signals are received by underwater transmitters, which record how often the shark enters the transmitter's area. Scientists are able to use the data collected by the underwater transmitters to track the travel habits of each individual tagged shark.

prey, and will eventually starve to death or become prey to other animals (since they cannot swim fast enough to escape potential predators). When people who eat shark fin soup are told about shark finning, they are often not made aware of the fact that the shark is unable to regrow its fin, and that sharks do not survive without their dorsal fins. Hunting mako sharks for their fins has led to a decline in their population. Shark finning has been outlawed in many countries, but in some areas, this barbaric practice is still legal.

In many countries, mako shark meat is considered a delicacy, and fishermen know that they are able to get a lot of money for killing mako sharks and selling the meat. Restaurants are willing to pay high prices for mako sharks. While there are limits on how many mako sharks fishermen are allowed to catch, these laws are often not followed. Fishermen can sell the mako shark meat

Sadly, some restaurants still serve shark fin soup.

to restaurants and report it to fishing officials as a different type of fish— no one except the restaurant and the fishermen know the truth. When a government does not know that sharks are being caught, there is little that they can do to stop these illegal actions.

Many fishermen also sell the mako shark's oil to be made into vitamins, as shark oil is marketed to help people with a variety of health issues. While fish oil can be beneficial, any kind of fish oil will provide the same positive

Mako sharks can get caught accidentally in fishing nets.

effects. Oil that comes from a shark has no benefit over oil that comes from another fish, such as tuna or salmon.

Mako sharks are often bycatch of commercial fishing operations. During commercial fishing, fishermen on boats throw out large nets to collect entire schools of fish at one time, rather than using a hook to catch individual fish. This practice is especially common for catching tuna, one of the staples of a mako shark's diet. While using a net makes a lot of sense because it catches many fish at one time, it is not the best practice for ocean creatures. Sometimes, animals the fishermen do not intend to catch—such as sharks, dolphins, and sea turtles—get stuck in the nets. Often, these nets do so much harm to the bycatch that they are unable to escape and eventually die. Even if fishermen do detangle the bycatch sharks from the net, it's likely that they will die because of their injuries. The net can cause large cuts in the shark's skin and gills, often to the point that the shark cannot recover.

Mako shark bycatch issues most commonly occur when fishing companies are attempting to catch swordfish and tuna, because mako sharks often prey upon both of these fish. Many companies are doing research on how to stop catching mako sharks while they are hunting for swordfish or tuna. Avoiding bycatch of makos can prove difficult because mako sharks approach their prey with such incredible speed. In fact, they swim faster than their prey! For fishermen to catch fish, they cannot travel faster than their targets. To avoid entangling mako sharks, a fishing boat would have to travel faster than the shark, which would also mean the boat would travel faster than the fish they are trying to catch. The fishermen would never make a catch! It's hard for companies to know when untagged mako sharks are near a school of fish. The more that scientists are able to tag mako fish, the better commercial fishing companies can be aware of when mako sharks are around and ready to hunt.

Some fishermen catch mako sharks for sport.

SPORT FISHING

Many recreational fishermen hunt the mako shark for sport. The most common areas in the world where recreational mako shark fishing occurs are off the coast of California, off the eastern coast of the United States, and off the coasts of Australia and New Zealand. Typically, sport fishermen do not use the shark's body for food or leather, it is simply a trophy. Many adventure fishing companies advertise shark fishing as a unique experience to participate in while traveling to seaside locations, as mako sharks tend to put on a show when they are caught. While the mako's breaching may look exciting to those who are fishing, in actuality, the shark is fighting for its life. Furthermore, mako sharks do not go down easily. Some makos that have been hooked have been known to break free of the hook and then jump on the boat to attack those on board. This dangerous aspect of sport fishing is what attracts many fishermen to these types of excursions. Since mako sharks will breach 10-20 ft. (about 3-6 m) out of the water in an attempt to free themselves from the fisherman's hook, others on board the boat often take pictures and video to share with friends, which many see as the highlight of their fishing trip. Allowing the shark to remain hooked and continue to jump typically ends poorly for the shark. Either it is unable to get free and further injures itself during the struggle (and the fisherman ends up killing the shark anyway), or it does get free, but it is left with a hook embedded in its mouth. A hook left in a shark's mouth can cause a variety of health problems for the shark, which can eventually lead to death. This is why companies that advertise that they will catch and release sharks are still hurting the shark population. It does not help the shark if you fatally injure it and then return it to the water.

Interestingly, the danger that comes with hunting mako sharks is exactly what drives so many people to attempt the hunt. After fishing, many fishermen will bring the shark's dead body back to the dock to show off to crowds of people. Many fishermen get a thrill out of hurting such a ferocious creature. Unfortunately, most mako sharks that are caught by fishermen have not reached full maturity. It's easier to catch smaller mako sharks since they weigh less and are less likely to be able to snap a fishing line or escape a fishing net. Killing young mako sharks means that they are being caught and killed without having the chance to reproduce, which makes it more likely that their population will continue to decline. It takes many years (up to six) for a mako shark to reach maturity and be able to reproduce.

SAVING THE MAKO SHARK: HOW TO HELP

In order for the mako shark population to grow and move away from their current vulnerable conservation status, it's important that people do their parts. There are many steps already being taken to protect makos, but there is more that needs to be done.

One way to contribute to conservation efforts is by writing to government officials in coastal states to ask them for stricter laws regarding mako shark fishing. In many states and countries, there are no laws to help keep the mako shark safe, and fishermen are able to hunt mako sharks without limitation. It's important that mako shark fishing be regulated so that the population can begin to grow again. While some government officials fear that regulating shark fishing could hurt the economy, sharks are actually more valuable alive. Companies that run cage diving and free-diving expeditions bring in more money than companies that hunt for sharks. Allowing people to experience mako sharks up close and alive makes a lot more money than selling shark body parts or food made from sharks.

Another way to keep mako sharks safe is by donating money to conservation organizations, such as the World Wildlife Fund, or WWF. The WWF (and other similar foundations) helps to fund research that allows scientists to learn more about endangered animals and how to keep them

Never buy jewelry made from shark bone or teeth.
It means a shark died for that piece of jewelry.

safe. (See the internet resources section in the back of this book to learn more about how to contribute.) On the WWF website you can adopt a shark, and the fee you pay will go toward research that helps shark populations grow. It's also a great idea to talk to your science teacher and see if you can work together as a class to fundraise the amount necessary to adopt an endangered animal!

If you go on vacation to an area where shark products (such as teeth, or clothes made from shark skin) are sold, it's important that you do not purchase these items. Often, they are not real, and if they are real, it means that a shark was killed for the item. When people stop purchasing items that are made from the bodies of sharks, fewer sharks will be killed. If you're interested in learning more about sharks, or getting up close to a shark, there are a variety of ways to do that without purchasing a part of a shark's body. (See chapter four for ways to interact with sharks.) It's also essential not to order meals in restaurants that feature shark meat or shark fins. If you're unsure if a dish contains shark meat, it's a good idea to ask your server for more details.

One of the most beneficial things that you can do to help sharks is simply to educate others about the important role sharks play in the ocean's ecosystem. Many people have the wrong idea about sharks. They believe that declining numbers of sharks in the ocean is a positive thing, and that the fewer sharks we have in the world, the safer it is for humans to swim and surf. This actually is not true. Sharks rarely attack people, and they are an important part of the ocean's ecosystem. Without sharks, other animal populations (such as squid and swordfish) would balloon out of control, and the ocean would become an unsafe place to swim for other reasons. Sharks also help keep the ocean healthy by preying upon weak and sick animals. If weak and sick animals were allowed to reproduce or spread disease, it could negatively affect the ocean's health. This would start a negative spiral that would affect many other aspects of ocean life. Talking to others about why sharks are important (and reminding people that sharks are unlikely to attack humans unless provoked or threatened) can be a useful way to help increase the number of these amazing creatures.

TEXT-DEPENDENT QUESTIONS:

1. Mako sharks are pelagic animals. What does this mean?

2. What is the mako shark's conservation status?

3. What's one way to help save mako sharks from becoming extinct?

RESEARCH PROJECT:

Many fishing companies are putting new practices into place to stop bycatch. Choose a fishing company and research what they are doing to reduce or stop bycatch from occurring.

WORDS TO UNDERSTAND:

cephalopod: Invertebrate animals that have tentacles, such as octopi and squid.

countershading: A type of camouflage exhibited by predators and prey alike in which the upper part of the animal is dark, and the underside is light.

endothermic: An animal that is able to warm and cool its body without changing its environment.

CHAPTER 3

THE MAKO SHARK'S DIET, BEHAVIOR, AND BIOLOGY

The mako shark is an apex predator. Being at the top of its food chain, the biggest threat to the mako shark's population is humans. At times, adult mako sharks will prey on juvenile mako sharks, but this does not happen often.

Humans are the biggest threat to mako sharks.

DIET

Mako sharks primarily eat cephalopods and bony fish. Cephalopods, such as squid and octopi, provide mako sharks with a great number of calories because of their high fat content. The more fat an animal has, the more energy a shark is able to get from it. It's crucial that mako sharks get high calorie meals, as they use lots of energy hunting and constantly swimming. Mako sharks also eat bony fish, such as swordfish, mackerel, tuna, and other sharks. While not as high in calories as cephalopods, bony fish still provide a high amount of fat because of the oil in their bodies. Makos have also been known to prey upon animals such as sea turtles, porpoises, and sea birds, but this is rare. It's likely that mako sharks only eat these animals when they are struggling to get enough to eat.

Mako sharks are incredible predators, but that does not mean that they are invincible. Often, mako sharks are discovered with their faces, gills, or bodies impaled by swordfish bills (the sword part of a swordfish's nose). Swordfish often put up a fight when attacked, but this does not seem to deter the mako shark from going after its favorite food. Many mako sharks have scarred faces because of frequent battles with various swordfish.

Mako sharks only need to hunt every other day.

With their high intelligence, it's likely that the sharks remember being hurt, but they are fearless enough to voluntarily put themselves in the same situation again anyway.

Mako sharks eat about 3 percent of their body weight each day, and it usually takes them about two days to digest a meal. This is noteworthy because it takes a lot of energy for mako sharks to hunt and swim! By only needing to hunt every other day, they are able to conserve valuable energy.

HUNTING

As cousins of the great white shark, it's no surprise that makos are excellent hunters. Unlike most other sharks, mako sharks do not rely on electroreception for hunting. Instead, they use their keen senses of vision, smell, and hearing to locate their prey. Their speed is also an important part of their hunting process, as it allows makos to sneak up on their prey undetected.

As pelagic animals that prey on other pelagic animals, mako sharks usually stay far away from the shoreline. The further away sharks go from the coast, the more difficult it is to find food. On the rare occasion that mako sharks do come near the shore, it is almost always because they are struggling to find food and must leave their comfort zone in order to keep themselves fed. In order to be successful hunters in the open ocean, mako sharks must be incredibly strategic in attacking their prey. The speed, intelligence, and fearless attitude of mako sharks make them hunters that nearly always get what they want.

It's common for mako sharks to attack entire schools of fish rather than attempting to single out one animal to eat. The larger the mako shark is, the larger (and more dangerous) its prey is. Baby and juvenile mako sharks will typically start out feeding on smaller animals such as bluefish, and they'll eventually graduate to attacking swordfish, porpoises, and dolphins. In order to attack larger animals, they need to have large teeth and lightning speed.

Scientists are still studying the way makos hunt.

It's difficult to say exactly how mako sharks hunt, as most marine biologists have never been able to watch an attack in the wild. Some scientists have placed underwater cameras to try to learn more about how mako sharks attack their prey. It's clear that mako sharks attack incredibly quickly, and that their fantastic eyesight is key in helping them locate their prey. They have large eyes that allow them to see well in areas where other animals are nearly blinded by darkness. Once a mako shark grabs ahold of its prey, it's nearly impossible for the prey to escape. It's likely that the shark either bites its prey in half or swallows it whole, allowing its large stomach to do the bulk of the work of digestion.

While the mako shark does not have any natural predators, it does attract parasites that can live on and harm its skin. Some smaller fish swim with mako sharks, eating the parasites off of their skin and keeping them healthy. Both species benefit from this relationship, known as symbiosis. Symbiosis is when two animals act in a way that benefits them both.

BIOLOGY

Mako sharks are quite large. The average mako shark weighs between 130 and 300 lbs. (60 to 135 kg), and measures approximately 10 ft. (3.2 m) in length. Females typically measure slightly larger than males. The largest mako shark ever recorded was 1,300 lbs. (600 kg), but most marine biologists believe that it's rare for mako sharks to grow to this size.

SHARKS

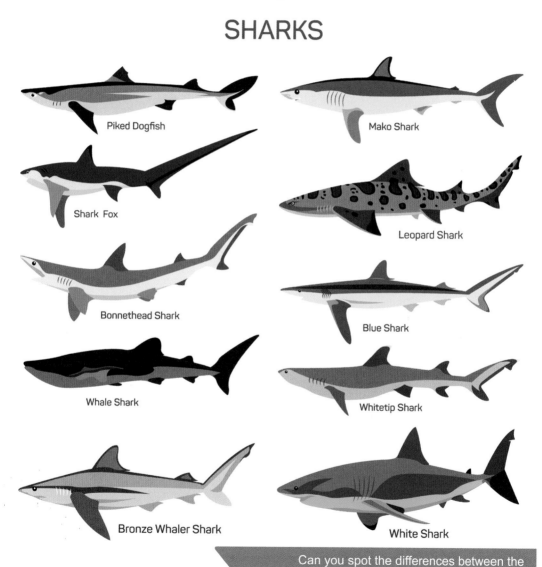

Piked Dogfish

Mako Shark

Shark Fox

Leopard Shark

Bonnethead Shark

Blue Shark

Whale Shark

Whitetip Shark

Bronze Whaler Shark

White Shark

Can you spot the differences between the mako shark and the other sharks?

Mako sharks have a long, cylindrical body with a large, muscular tail—much larger than the tails of most sharks. Their coloring is typical of animals that exhibit countershading, as the top of their bodies is a bright, metallic blue color, and their bellies fade to a bright white. Large mako sharks typically have a larger area of blue coloring than smaller mako sharks, with their blue scales extending into areas that would be white in a smaller shark. Countershading is important when it comes to hunting and staying safe from predators. When viewed from above the water, mako sharks are very difficult to see, as their bright blue dorsal side blends in with the ocean's surface. When viewed from below, makos are also quite difficult to see, as their white bellies help them to blend in with the sky above. Young mako sharks are easily distinguishable from older mako sharks by a black splotch on their noses that usually fades with age.

The mako's smile looks fierce.

Watch as these marine biologists find and tag a mako shark to learn more about its migration patterns, behavior, and preferred habitat.

The mako shark's jaw is bowl shaped, and filled with many rows of sharp teeth. In fact, there are twelve to thirteen rows of teeth in the upper jaw and eleven to twelve rows of teeth in the lower jaw. The teeth are large and triangular, and on both the upper and lower jaw, the teeth point inward. This hook-like shape makes it nearly impossible for prey to escape once the mako shark takes a bite. One of the hallmarks of the mako shark is that the teeth of the lower jaw are visible even when the shark's mouth is closed, creating a permanently intimidating appearance!

Mako sharks are built for speed. Their unique body shape is streamlined—like a torpedo—to allow them to glide through the water. Their long, cylindrical snouts create a point that makes it easy for them to cut through the ocean water with as little drag as possible. Think about how difficult it is to run through the water compared with running on land. It's harder to run in water because of something called drag—the ability of the water to create resistance. A mako shark's body is shaped to provide the least amount of drag possible. Its large, muscular tail is also imperative for propelling it through the water quickly. Most sharks have tails that are uneven—the top half is usually longer than the bottom half. With mako sharks, the tail is a bit different, as the halves are nearly identical. Their strong, even tails allow the mako shark to reach higher speeds than most sharks. Also, the evenness of the top and bottom halves allows the mako to propel itself through the water with less effort than if its tail were uneven. A mako shark's tail has a fleshy ridge called a caudal keel. The caudal keel allows the mako shark to transfer energy from the muscles in its body to its tail. This, paired with the mako's high metabolic rate (ability to create energy inside its body), creates incredible speed.

Some fish have a swim bladder, a special organ that helps them to stay afloat without having to put in much effort. The mako shark does not have a swim bladder, and therefore, must swim constantly (even when resting) so that it does not sink. When a mako shark swims, it usually leaves its mouth open, which allows water to run over its five large gills on either side of its head. These gills work to pull oxygen out of the water, just like your lungs pull oxygen out of the air to keep you alive. The oxygen is then transferred to the shark's bloodstream and is distributed throughout its body to fuel its heart and other muscles. If mako sharks stop swimming, it's likely that they will be unable to pull oxygen out of the water and will suffocate. This is another reason that mako sharks must eat high calorie meals—to keep up the energy required to constantly swim!

While most sharks are ectothermic (cold-blooded), mako sharks are endothermic (warm-blooded). This means that they are able to regulate their body temperature just like people do, cooling themselves down if they get too hot and warming themselves up if they get too cold. This allows them to keep their bodies at a comfortable temperature regardless of the water around them. It also helps them use their energy efficiently, which contributes to their speed while hunting. Most fish lose a significant amount of body heat through their gills, but the mako shark does not. Typically, a mako shark's body temperature is about ten degrees warmer than the temperature of

Mako sharks must swim constantly to stay alive.

the surrounding water. The ability to control their own body temperature allows mako sharks to maintain a high level of activity, which gives them an advantage over their cold-blooded prey, such as tuna, swordfish, other sharks, and sea turtles.

LIFE SPAN

While mako sharks cannot survive in captivity, marine biologists are doing their best to study the shark's life span in the wild. It's important to note that all life spans are estimated. It's difficult to know exactly how long sharks live when no one has ever been able to observe a single shark for its entire life.

LONGFIN VS. SHORTFIN MAKO SHARK: WHAT'S THE DIFFERENCE?

There are two different categories of mako shark: longfin and shortfin. Of course, the first clear difference is the size of their pectoral fins. Longfin makos also have larger eyes than their short-finned relatives. Shortfin mako sharks are much more common than longfin mako sharks—longfins weren't even described as a separate species until 1966. Longfin mako sharks are likely to swim a little bit deeper than shortfins, but they are also considered a pelagic species. Longfin mako sharks also tend to be a bit larger than shortfin mako sharks. Their habitats differ slightly as well—longfin mako sharks tend to swim exclusively in tropical waters, while shortfin makos swim in tropical, subtropical, and temperate waters. Much more is known about shortfin mako sharks, as they are more common, swim closer to the surface, and are easier for scientists to study.

Male mako sharks live to be around twenty-nine years old, while female mako sharks usually live to be around thirty-two years old. It's likely that there are mako sharks that are older than these estimates. As mako sharks age, their vertebrae (the tiny segments that make up their spines) grow rings, just like a tree grows a ring in its trunk each year. When scientists find a mako shark that has died, they are able to study these vertebrae rings to find out how many years the shark lived. It's possible that some mako sharks live even longer, but since scientists cannot estimate how old a shark is until it has died, it's difficult to know for sure. Mako sharks seem to be living longer and longer in the years that scientists have been studying them, and no one is quite sure why this phenomenon is happening.

TEXT-DEPENDENT QUESTIONS:

1. How does countershading help keep mako sharks safe?

2. How long do mako sharks live?

3. What are the physical characteristics of the mako shark that allow it to be such a fast swimmer?

RESEARCH PROJECT:

The mako shark is one of four warm-blooded sharks. Research the three other types of warm-blooded sharks, and learn more about how their speeds compare to that of the mako shark.

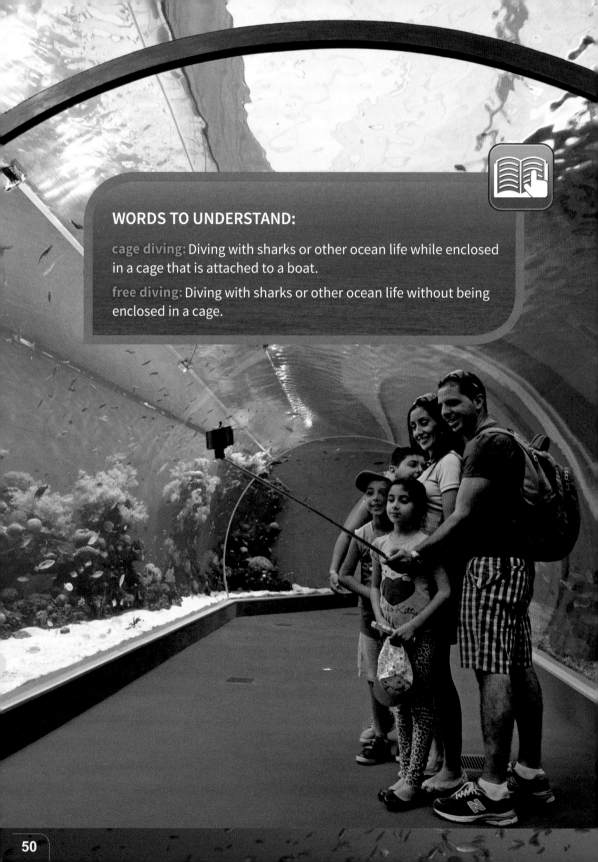

WORDS TO UNDERSTAND:

cage diving: Diving with sharks or other ocean life while enclosed in a cage that is attached to a boat.

free diving: Diving with sharks or other ocean life without being enclosed in a cage.

CHAPTER 4

ENCOUNTERING A MAKO SHARK

If you're interested in diving with mako sharks, there are many places that allow you to do so! The most popular locations for diving with mako sharks are off the coasts of California, South Africa, and the Maldives. There are a few different options when it comes to encountering a mako shark face-to-face.

CAGE DIVING

Cage diving is the most common way to encounter sharks. It's crucial that you cage dive with a licensed, experienced professional. While mako sharks are unlikely to attack humans, it's still necessary to cage dive with someone who has experience with these amazing animals. When cage diving, you'll board a boat at a dock, and the captain and crew will drive the boat out to a location known for mako sharks. Remember, this location may be fairly far from shore, as mako sharks are pelagic and unlikely to swim near the coast. As you

Diving in a cage like this is one way to see a mako shark.

arrive at the dive location, your captain and crew will likely chum the waters, meaning they will add a mixture of blood, bones, and fish pieces to the water around the boat. Chumming the waters is illegal in some areas, so there is a chance that your captain will be able to attract sharks in a different way.

Safety is key—the boat's crew will go over a few rules with you to make sure you stay safe. You'll receive instructions to keep all body parts—including hands, fingers, and toes—inside the cage, so that it's not possible for you to get harmed by the shark. Your boat crew will also explain to you how to let them know if you need to come out of the water if you become scared or feel unsafe.

After mako sharks begin to swim around the boat, the crew will help you get into a wetsuit and will teach you how to use an apparatus that will allow you to breathe while underwater. A cage with metal bars will be placed in the ocean near the surface, and will be attached to the boat with a steel chain. You will step into the

Before diving, you'll be given diving equipment to use.

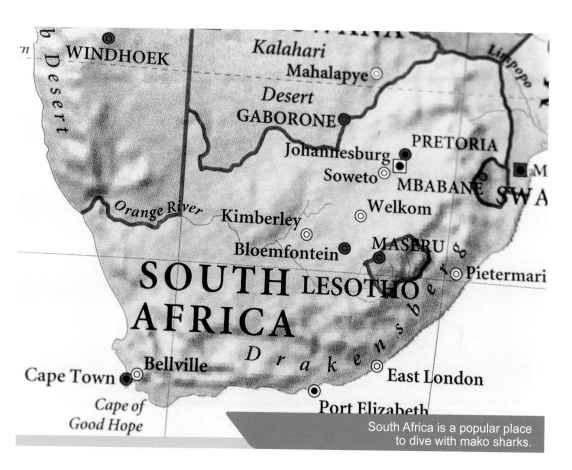

South Africa is a popular place to dive with mako sharks.

cage and the top will be closed. Often, you'll be able to get into the cage with a friend or family member, as many of the cages are large enough to accommodate a small group. After you're in the cage, the boat crew will close and latch the top of the cage, and you will be lowered below the ocean's surface, breathing through the apparatus provided. As you're lowered into the water, mako sharks will swim around the cage, and you'll get to see what they look like up close.

Free diving is one way to see sharks, such as this diver with a mako and a blue shark.

FREE DIVING

Feeling brave? Many adventure companies offer **free diving** with mako sharks. Makos tend to be a little bit shy. Most adventure companies will guarantee that you'll see sharks on your trip, but it's unlikely that they'll guarantee that you'll see a mako, as they are unpredictable. Remember, if you'd like to dive with sharks, it's important that you do so with a trained professional. This is not an activity that you should attempt on your own.

According to many divers, mako sharks are some of the scariest sharks to swim with because of their speed and fast, twitchy movements. It's essential to remember that your diving team will be trained in the behavior of mako sharks and will be able to alert you if dangerous or threatening behavior is beginning to occur.

When free diving, your boat crew and captain will take you out into the open ocean, usually about 30 mi. (48.3 km) miles away from the shore. Since mako sharks do not come near the coastline, it's necessary to meet them in their natural habitat to increase the chances that you'll get to swim with them.

When the boat gets to an area known for sharks, the boat crew will chum the water, the same as if you were cage diving. You'll be given a wetsuit and a breathing apparatus that will allow you to breathe underwater. Typically, members of the crew will get in the water first to ensure that the sharks are not behaving in an aggressive manner. The boat crew knows the behaviors to

Never dive with sharks alone.

watch for to predict if the sharks are likely to become aggressive or not. If the sharks appear to be calm, the crew members will give permission for others to join them in the water.

Your boat crew will give you instructions on how to act in the water—how close you can get to the sharks, any behaviors you should avoid, and how long you'll be staying in the water. It's important to pay close attention to these instructions and ask questions if anything is unclear.

IS IT SAFE TO SWIM WITH SHARKS?
As long as you use a reputable company, swimming with sharks is very safe. Your guides are trained professionals who know how to watch out for signs of aggression. In areas with a large tourism industry, it's likely that sharks are used to divers and enjoy the treats that the shark diving boats bring. Remember that diving with sharks alone is not a good idea, but diving when guided by a reputable adventure company can be a safe, fun way to view sharks in their natural habitat.

This diver made the bad decision to dive alone, and narrowly escaped a mako shark.

As you swim with the sharks, the crew will keep an eye on you and let you know if there's something exciting to see, but for the most part, you'll be on your own, enjoying the underwater show put on by the sharks.

MAKO SHARKS IN CAPTIVITY

Like many sharks, mako sharks do not thrive in captivity. The longest survival time for a mako shark in captivity is only five days. Since mako sharks are pelagic animals, they need open space to swim. When pelagic sharks are confined to an aquarium, they have trouble navigating the boundaries, such as walls and glass. They tend to run into these obstacles, injuring themselves. After a few days, many sharks in captivity refuse to eat, become weak, and eventually die. While it may sound exciting to see a shark in an aquarium, it's important to remember that sharks are wild animals that must be cared for properly.

 TEXT-DEPENDENT QUESTIONS:

1. How do people breathe while cage diving?

2. How far away from land is it necessary to go to see mako sharks?

3. Why are you unlikely to see mako sharks in captivity?

 RESEARCH PROJECT:

Mako sharks do not survive in captivity, but some sharks do well in aquariums. Find out which sharks are able to thrive in captivity, and explain what makes them different from mako sharks.

SERIES GLOSSARY OF KEY TERMS

Apparatus: A device or a collection of tools that are used for a specific purpose. A diving apparatus helps you breathe under water.

Barbaric: Something that is considered unrefined or uncivilized. The idea of killing sharks just for their fins can be seen as barbaric.

Buoyant: Having the ability to float. Not all sharks are buoyant. They need to swim to stay afloat.

Camouflage: To conceal or hide something. Sharks' coloring often helps camouflage them from their prey.

Chum: A collection of fish guts and fish remains thrown into the ocean to attract sharks. Divers will often use chum to help attract sharks.

Conservation: The act of preserving or keeping things safe. Conservation is important in keeping sharks and oceans safe from humans.

Decline: To slope down or to decrease in number. Shark populations are on the decline due to human activity.

Delicacy: Something, particularly something to eat, that is very special and rare. Shark fin soup is seen as a delicacy in some Asian countries, but it causes a decline in shark populations.

Expedition: A type of adventure that involves travel for a specific purpose. Traveling to a location specifically to see sharks would be considered an expedition.

Ferocious: Describes something that is mean, fierce, or extreme. Sharks often look ferocious because of their teeth and the way they attack their prey.

Finning: The act of cutting off the top (dorsal) fin of a shark specifically to sell for meat. Sharks cannot swim without all of their fins, so finning leads to a shark's death.

Frequent: To go somewhere often. Sharks tend to frequent places where there are lots of fish.

Ft.: An abbreviation for feet or foot, which is a unit of measurement. It is equal to 12 inches or about .3 meters.

Indigenous: Native to a place or region.

Intimidate: To scare or cause fear. Sharks can intimidate other fish and humans because of their fierce teeth.

Invincible: Unable to be beaten or killed. Sharks seem to be invincible, but some species are endangered.

KPH: An abbreviation for kilometers per hour, which is a metric unit of measurement for speed. One kilometer is equal to approximately .62 miles.

M: An abbreviation for meters, which is a metric unit of measurement for distance. One meter is equal to approximately 3.28 feet.

Mi.: An abbreviation for miles, which is a unit of measurement for distance. One mile is equal to approximately 1.61 kilometers.

Migrate: To move from one place to another. Sharks often migrate from cool to warm water for several different reasons.

MPH: An abbreviation for miles per hour, which is a unit of measurement for speed. One mile is equal to approximately 1.61 kilometers.

Phenomenon: Something that is unusual or amazing. Seeing sharks in the wild can be quite a phenomenon.

Prey: Animals that are hunted for food—either by humans or other animals. It can also mean the act of hunting.

Reputable: Something that is considered to be good or to have a good reputation. When diving with sharks, it is important to find a reputable company that has been in business for a long time.

Staple: Something that is important in a diet. Vegetables are staples in our diet, and fish is a staple in sharks' diets.

Strategy: A plan or method for achieving a goal. Different shark species have different hunting strategies.

Temperate: Something that is not too extreme such as water temperature. Temperate waters are not too cold or too hot.

Tentacles: Long arms on an animal that are used to move or sense objects. Octopi have tentacles that help them catch food.

Vulnerable: Something that is easily attacked. We don't think of sharks as being vulnerable, but they are when they're being hunted by humans.

INDEX

FURTHER READING

Lockyer, John. *All About Sharks*. Huntington Beach: Teacher Created Materials, 2008.

Muller, Michael. *Sharks*. Worthing: Littlehampton Book Services, 2016.

Musgrave, Ruth. *Sharks: All the Shark Facts, Photos, and Fun That You Can Sink Your Teeth Into!* Washington: National Geographic, 2011.

Parker, Steve. *The Encyclopedia of Sharks*. Richmond Hill: Firefly Books, 2008.

Schrieber, Anne. *Sharks!* Washington: National Geographic, 2008.

INTERNET RESOURCES

http://cnso.nova.edu:
The Halmos College of Natural Sciences and Oceanography provides shark videos and shark activity maps.

http://cnso.nova.edu/sharktracking:
The Guy Harvey Research Institute (GHRI) Shark Tracking partners with the Halmos College of Natural Sciences and Oceanography in tracking and recording shark activity. The GHRI dedicates its resources to the preservation of marine life, including sharks.

http://www.defenders.org/sharks/basic-facts:
The Defenders of Wildlife site offers fast facts about the diet, habitat, range, and behavior of a variety of sharks.

https://www.discovery.com/tv-shows/shark-week:
The Discovery Channel's Shark Week site provides page after page of helpful shark information, informative videos, and stories of close encounters with all types of sharks.

http://saveourseas.com:
The Save Our Seas Foundation focuses their efforts specifically on saving sharks and rays. Their website includes shark facts, a newsletter, and details about how to help save sharks and rays.

http://www.worldwildlife.org:
The World Wildlife Fund provides a variety of resources for learning about and supporting vulnerable, threatened, and endangered animals.

AT A GLANCE

200 ft.

Hammerhead Sharks
Length: 20 ft. (6.1 m)
Swim Depth: 262 ft. (80 m)
Lifespan: 20+ years

400 ft.

Bull Sharks
Length: 11.1 ft. (3.4 m)
Swim Depth: 492 ft. (150 m)
Lifespan: 18+ years

Rays
Length: 8.2 ft. (2.5 m)
Swim Depth: 656 ft. (200 m)
Lifespan: 30 years

600 ft.

800 ft.

Great White Sharks
Length: 19.6 ft. (6 m)
Swim Depth: 820 ft. (250 m)
Lifespan: 30 years

Blue Sharks
Length: 12.5 ft. (3.8 m)
Swim Depth: 1,148 ft. (350 m)
Lifespan: 20 years

1,000 ft.

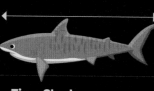

1,200 ft.

Tiger Sharks
Length: 11.5 ft. (3.5 m)
Swim Depth: 1148 ft. (350 m)
Lifespan: 50 years

Thresher Sharks
Length: 18.7 ft. (5.7 m)
Swim Depth: 1200 ft. (366 m)
Lifespan: 50 years

1,400 ft.

Mako Sharks
Length: 13.1 ft. (4 m)
Swim Depth: 1,640 ft. (500 m)
Lifespan: 32 years

1,600 ft.

1,800 ft.

Source: www.iucnredlist.org

PHOTO CREDITS

EDUCATIONAL VIDEO LINKS

Chapter 1
How are Mako sharks able to swim so fast? Watch this video and find out:
http://x-qr.net/1Dhb

Chapter 2
This video shows the variety of animal life that lives in the pelagic zone:
http://x-qr.net/1EkU

Chapter 3
Watch as these marine biologists find and tag a mako: http://x-qr.net/1DTn

Chapter 4
This diver made the bad decision to dive alone, and narrowly escaped a mako shark: http://x-qr.net/1E8t

AUTHOR'S BIOGRAPHY

Elizabeth Roseborough is a former college, high school, and middle school biology instructor. When not visiting her favorite Caribbean islands, Elizabeth spends her time with her husband, son, and their fur babies, Titan and Stella, at their home in Dayton, Ohio.